*treacherous
piercing
thorn*

treacherous piercing thorn

the collected poems of
Lloyd Nelson Wood

edited by Tim Wood

OHWPRESS

Colorado Springs   OHWpress.com

A previous edition of this book was published by Press Wood Ink.

TREACHEROUS PIERCING THORN
©2002, 2008 by Tim Wood.

The images contained in the lyrics and maps section are believed to be in the public domain. All other rights reserved. No part of this book may be used or reproduced in any manner whatsoever without written permission except in the case of brief quotations embodied in critical articles and reviews, and use of the noted images. For information, address OHWPress, 4419 Centennial Blvd #309, Colorado Springs CO 80907

First OHWpress Edition, 2008

ISBN-13: 978-0-9822193-0-0
ISBN-10: 0-9822193-0-X

for everyone who has had
words cut
and love
and burn
and save

especially the poets

Contents

Introduction to The First Edition	ix
Introduction to the Second Edition	xi
Rhymes of Ralphie	1
Loved and Lost	5
Confessions of Failure	13
To Evelyn on the First Anniversary	17
No Smile Tonight	19
Where's Old Doc	23
Christmas 1941	27
In the Spring	29
The Cedar Chest	33
To Rose on her Fourteenth Birthday	35
To Jencie Rusco, on her Ninth Birthday	39
To Jackie Rusco, on her Twelfth Birthday	41
Christmas 1942	43
Untitled	45
To Walk with Me	47
Jackie Loves poor old Me	53
To Eva on her Birthday	57
Walking with Joycie	59
Now and Forever	61
Christmas 1945	63
To Jencie Rusco	65
Three little girls and I	69
To Dorothy	73
To Dorothy Morales	75
Tune, My Old Kentucky Home	77
A girl less day	81
To Martha Ann on her Tenth Birthday	83

Introduction to The First Edition

At the wake for Lloyd Nelson Wood's son Robert —my grandfather— I spent hours looking through photo albums and talking to the family, trying to learn something beyond the sketchy things I could remember about my family. I suspect I'm going to be learning for a long time to come. But, one thing I did find out that day was that my poetry wasn't some strange lark in the family. It turns out that poetry is something of a family curse. The wake was held at the house of Mary Wood. After a while she handed me an old three ring binder with the poems in this collection. The first work on this collection —scanning the photos on the cover— was done at the wake.

Thanks go out to the people and resources that made this project possible. First, I have to thank Mary Wood for the originals for these poems, the images throughout and serving as general project muse. Charles Wood provided invaluable assistance with difficult spots and references in the originals. Any number of family members contributed biographical information or made contributions I've long forgotten. The search engine google.com and lyric crawler www.joesharp.com were very helpful in clarifying references; especially in the Music and References section. Thanks to my faithful stuffed mascot Phyl for watching over my computer.

For the most part, I kept things as he wrote them. There are some cases where I made minor changes for consistency, to clarify a line, or because I wasn't certain what was in the original. Needless to say, any mistakes are mine and not those of anyone who helped out with this project.

This book was brought to you by the letter/cat Q. It's dedicated to Lloyd Nelson Wood's Great-Great Grand Daughter Serene Devin Wood (Devin means poet in Celtic). We hope she will takeup a pen someday, too.

Introduction to the Second Edition

The second edition consists of a number of corrections. But, then again what second edition doesn't? The book now closes with additional material including lyrics of the songs referenced in the poems. The poems are now in chronological order making clear the gap from late 1943 until late 1945.

treacherous
piercing
thorn

Rhymes of Ralphie   Spring 1940

We all are looking forward to,
A sweeter by and by,
When grand pa's little Ralphie boy,
Will laugh instead of cry.
He'll have to quit his hewing up,
And keep his blanket clean,
If he intends to rock a by,
With petty aunt Lorraine.
He shurely is entitled to,
Some pleasure out of life,
I hope he'll pucker up his mouth,
And play old grand pa's fife.

They soon will cease to cook his milk,
He'll like it better raw,
Whether its from old Dobbin Syrup,
Or Sandy in the Craw.
The day he had his picture took,
He looked so tiny there,
Where mamma had him all proped up,
In grandma's old arm chair.
To see him sitting in his pen,
Surrounded by his toys,
Brings back once more the memories sweet,
Of by gone Christmas joys.

Spring 1940

Rhymes of Ralphie

We all are looking forward to,
A Sweeter by and by,
When grandpa's little Ralphie boy,
Will laugh instead of cry.

He'll have to quit his pewking up,
And keep his blanket clean,
If he intends to rock a by,
With pretty Aunt Lorraine.

He surely is entitled to,
Some pleasures out of life,
I hope he'll pucker up his mouth,
And play old grandpa's fife.

They soon will cease to cook his milk,
He'll like it better raw,
Whether it's from old Dobbin's Diner,
Or sandy in the craw.

The day he had his picture took,
He looked so tiny there,
when mamma had him all propped up,
In grandma's old armchair.

To see him sitting in his pen,
Surrounded by his toys,
Brings back once more the memories sweet,
Of bygone Christmas joys.

We took him to a church one night,
The Oneness Pentacost,
And hoped the funny doings there,
Would keep his mind engrossed.

He went around among the folks,
And yelled with lusty lungs,
When mamma tried to make him stop,
He screeched in unknown tongues.

He paid no heed at all when asked,
To cease his roguish ways,
Altho he knew by doing so,
Would please the Bonnie Brays.

He ran and rolled all up and down,
The humble saw dust trail,
And kissed the girls most shamelessly,
Before the alters rail.

While prayers were being offered up,
He'd clap his hands and dance,
Where others got the Holy Ghost,
He stood and wet his pants.

The preacher said this little child,
So innocent and free,
Is one our loving Savior called,
Saying "come unto me"

Do not dispise this gentle soul,
Or scold and rudely shake,
For Jesus said "its such as he,
That Heavens kingdom make"

We took him to a Church one night,
The Oneness Pentecost,
And hoped the funny doings there,
Would keep his mind engrossed.

He went around among the folks,
And yelled with lusty lungs,
When mamma tried to make his stop,
He screeched in unknown tongues.

He paid no heed at all when asked,
To cease his roguish ways,
Altho he knew by doing so,
Would please the Bonnie Brays.

He ran and rolled all up and down,
The humble saw dust trail,
And kissed the girls most shamelessly,
Before the alter rail.

While prayers were being offered up,
He'd clap his hands and dance,
Where others got the Holy Ghost,
He stood and wet his pants.

The preacher said this little child,
So innocent and free,
Is one our loving Savior called,
Saying "come onto me"

Do not despise this gentle call,
Or scold and rudely shake,
For Jesus said "it's such as he
that Heaven's Kingdom make."

Loved and Lost   May 1940

I lie and muse at break of day,
Of one I chanced to meet,
Who wrote into my dreary life,
A chapter sad and sweet.

Yes, as we journey down the path,
Of times circitous way,
The chapters in our book of life,
Are written day by day.

Some by ourselves with studied course,
And thoughtfull actions planed,
While others are imprinted there,
By oft another hand.

Great masters since the dawn of time,
Have dwelt upon this theme,
Great thesess on its why's and how,
Thru endless pages stream.

I shall not wander far afield,
Nor strain my feeble mind,
By searching for some beauties rare,
That they had failed to find.

I quote a saying from some bard,
Who, I can not recall,
"T'was better to have loved and lost,
Than never loved at all."

May 1940

Loved and Lost

I lie and muse at break of day,
If one I chanced to meet,
Who wrote into my dreary life,
A chapter sad and sweet.

Yes, as we journey down the path,
Of time's circuitous way,
The chapters in our book of life,
Are written day by day.

Some by ourselves with studied course,
And thoughtful actions planned,
While others are imprinted there,
By oft another hand.

Great masters since the dawn of time,
Have dwelt upon this theme,
Great theses on it's why's and how,
Thru endless pages stream.

I shall not wander far afield,
Nor strain my feeble mind,
By searching for some beauties rare,
That they had failed to find.

I quote a saying from some bard,
Who, I can not recall,
"T'was better to have loved and lost,
Than never loved at all."

He must have meant the first romance,
When innocence did reign,
The lovers walked in nakedness,
Thru Eden's fair domain.

For Adam shurely must have loved,
They tell me that he lost,
And that its up to even us,
To pay the fearfull cost.

I would not mind to meet my due,
Could I but have attained,
The fullness of that recompense,
The poor old fellow gained.

For Adam as we understand,
Did realy fall from grace,
Partaking of the favors of,
The mother of our race.

I'd fall asleep a hundred years,
And all my ribs donate,
If I could have the pleasure of,
Pasessing such a mate.

But, realy his accomplishment,
Was not so great a feat,
Remember, he had only
With the devil to compete

He must have meant the first romance,
When innocence did reign,
The lovers walked in nakedness,
Thru Eden's fair domains.

For Adam surely must have loved,
They tell me that he lost,
And that it's up to even us,
To pay the fearful cost.

I would not mind to meet my due,
Could I but have attained,
The fullness of that recompense,
The poor old fellow gained.

For Adam as we understand,
Did really fall from grace,
Partaking of the favors of,
The mother of our race.

I'd fall asleep a hundred years,
And all my ribs donate,
If I could have the pleasure of,
Possessing such a mate.

But, really his accomplishment,
Was not so great a feat,
Remember, he had only
With the devil to compete.

So much for ancient romancing,
In that enchanted clime,
Now let's get back to what took place,
In our more modern time.
I fell in love in Autumn late,
Of nineteen hundred nine,
With all the thrills companion to,
That ecstacy devine.

Yes, I was slow to reach that state,
Of which poets sweetly sing,
The proper time to fall in love,
Is in the budding spring.

The fair one I so much admired,
Oft told me I was slow,
And could not hope to make the grade,
By peeping on in low.

The thought that I might lose the prize,
So filled my heart with fear,
I tried at once to shift in high,
And stripped out every gear.

For I was taught there strictly must,
No morals be outraged,
That I must never kiss a girl,
Until we were engaged.

So much for ancient romancing,
In that enchanted clime,
Now let's get back to what took place,
In our more modern time.

I fell in love in Autumn late,
Of nineteen hundred nine,
With all the thrills companion to,
That ecstasy divine.

Yes, I was slow to reach that state,
Of which poets sweetly sing,
The proper time to fall in love,
Is in the budding spring.

The fair one I so much admired,
Oft told me I was slow,
And could not hope to make the grade,
By keeping on in tow.

The thought that I might lose the prize,
So filled my heart with fear,
I tried at once to shift in high,
And stripped out every gear.

For I was taught there strictly must,
No morals be outraged,
That I must never kiss a girl,
Until we were engaged.

It's hard for us now to conceive,
Such courtship, quaintly tame,
It would have worked out perfectly,
Had she been taught the same.

So now I took the notion to,
Her bosom gently feel,
And thought I might by doing so,
Build up my sex appeal.

Right there I learned that sex appeal,
Which I so much desired,
Is of itself an inborn trait,
And can not be acquired.

What happened, oh, well never mind,
All that was long ago,
For I was strong and active then,
Could dodge or take a blow.

I then decided that my suit,
No longer would I press,
But still I must forever adore,
Her slender loveliness.

I sit and muse at eventide,
For truly I am glad,
She wrote into my life forlorn,
That chapter sweet and sad.

It's hard for us now to conceive,
Such courtship, quaintly tame,
It would have worked out perfectly,
Had she been taught the same.

So now I took the notion to,
Her bosom gently feel,
And thought I might by doing so,
Build up my sex appeal.

Right there I learned that sex appeal,
Which I so much desired,
Is of itself an inborn trait,
And can not be acquired.

What happened, oh, well never mind,
All that was long ago,
For I was strong and active then,
Could dodge or take a blow.

I then decided that my suit,
No longer would I press,
But still I must forever adore,
Her slender loveliness.

I sit and muse at eventide,
For truly am I glad,
She wrote into my life forlorn,
That chapter sweet and sad.

Confession of failure.   Spring 1941

Here's to the ladies, loving and lovely,
Pride of creation's blessings so rare,
Given for man to be a companion,
Helping him all life's burdens to bear.

Taken from man and fashioned in beauty,
Destined to fill his greatest desire,
In the begining perfect and faultless,
Seemingly making all things entire.

All of my lonely life I have loved them,
Loving them still as older I grow,
Now I must close by begging their pardon,
Far to presume their love I could know.

Other men around me gathered the jewels,
Allways appeared to konquer with ease,
What'er I tried was allways a failure,
Never could seem their fancy to please.

Little I knew of feminine nature,
Nothing at all of feminine wiles,
Only I longed for kindred emotion
Sharing alike thru life's weary trials.

Oh; what I missed by loosing my mother
Who better than she could love, comfy teach
Gives of herself eternal devotion,
Farther than any other can reach.

Spring 1941

Confessions of Failure

Here's to the ladies, loving and lovely,
Pride of creation's blessings so rare,
Given for man to be a companion,
Helping him all life's burdens to bear.

Taken from man and fashioned in beauty,
Destined to fill his greatest desire,
In the beginning, perfect and faultless,
Seemingly making all things entire.

All of my lonely life I have loved them,
Loving them still as older I grow,
Now I must close by begging their pardon,
For to presume their love I could know.

Other men around me gathered the jewels,
Always appeared to conquer with ease,
What'er I tried was always a failure,
Never could seem their fancy to please.

Little I knew of feminine nature,
Nothing at all of feminine wiles,
Only I longed for kindred emotion,
Sharing alike thru life's weary trials.

Oh: what I missed by losing my mother
Who better than she could love's causes teach
Gives of herself eternal devotion,
Farther than any other can reach.

Oh! may there be some spirit of Eden,
One whom the serpent has not beguiled,
Down thru the ages for me is waiting,
That with my own to be reconciled.

Oh! may there be some spirit of Eden,
One whom the serpent has not beguiled,
Down thru the ages for me is waiting,
That with my own to be reconciled.

To Evelyn on the first anniversary, Mar. 23, 1941

Again as time another turn,
Around the circle swings,
The twenty third of March no doubt,
A pleasant memory brings.

For was it not a year ago,
You made a solemn vow,
Pledging with all your worldly goods,
Each other to endow.

I will renew the same old wish,
With every passing year,
That happiness may be your lot
With joys we hold most dear.

If old acquaintanceship I claim,
Don't think me over bold,
The acquaintance may be somewhat new
But truly I am old.

I truly wish and fondly hope,
With loneliness my lot,
That all acquaintance, old or new,
May never be forgot.

Mar 23, 1941

To Evelyn on the First Anniversary

Again as time another turn,
Around the circle swings,
The twenty-third of March no doubt,
A pleasant memory brings.

For was it not a year ago,
You made a solemn vow,
Pledging with all your worldly goods,
Each other to endow.

I will renew the same old wish,
With every passing year,
That happiness may be your lot
With joys we hold most dear.

If old acquaintanceship I claim,
Don't think me over bold,
The acquaintance may be somewhat new
But truly I am old.

I truly wish and fondly hope,
With loneliness my lot,
That all acquaintance, old or new,
May never be forgot.

No Smile to night   late Aug. 1941

One evening when summer was nearly spent,
You could feel the approach of fall,
Alone by myself on a bench I sat,
In the Salvation Army Hall.

The setting of course you all well know,
It is such a familiar scene,
The uniformed lassie, so sweet and fair,
With the jingling tambourine.

Why was it I went in those summer eves,
To a meeting of music and prayer,
It was often I went to obtain relief,
From the every day worries and care.

When asked if the stains of my life were cleansed,
By Gilead's Healing Balm,
I answered by quoting verse sixty three,
Of the hundred and nineteenth psalm.

My part in the service was small indeed,
Producing a jingling sound,
By dropping a coin in the tambourine,
When the lassie so sweet came around.

Tu this was the part I most enjoyed,
When my gift in the pan was laid,
Receiving a smile and a "God bless you"
From the Salvation Army maid.

Late Aug. 1941

No Smile Tonight

One evening when summer was nearly spent,
You could feel the approach of fall,
Alone by myself in a bunch I sat,
In the Salvation Army Hall.

The setting of course you all well know,
It is such a familiar scene,
The uniformed lassie, so sweet and fair,
With the jingling tambourine.

Why was it I went in those summer eves,
To a meeting of music and prayer,
It was often I went to obtain relief,
From the every day worries and care.

When asked if the stains of my life were cleansed,
By Gilead's Healing Balm,
I answered by quoting verse sixty-three,
Of the hundred and nineteenth psalm.

My part in the service was small indeed,
Producing a jingling sound,
By dropping a coin in the tambourine,
When the lassie so sweet came around.

For this was the part I most enjoyed,
When my gift in the pan was laid.
Receiving a smile and a "God bless you"
Form the Salvation Army maid.

A generous feeling came o're me there,
As the lassie came down the aisle,
I shurely was able to night to give,
A dime for a chulset smile.

The gift was as welcome as any could be,
But the giver was old and gray,
She gave me no smile as the coin chapped in
But turned her sweet face away.

Still worried and lonely and filled with care,
Oppressed by the same old stairs,
And feel I can visit that hall no more,
Or sit on that bench again.

Oh! lassie press on in your noble cause,
With you I will ever agree,
No more to expect you to waste your smiles,
On a poor old sinner like me.

A generous feeling came o're me there,
As the lassie came down the aisle,
I surely was able tonight to give,
A dime for a dulcet smile.

The gift was as welcome as any could be,
But the giver was old and gray,
She gave me no smile as the coin dropped in
But turned her sweet face away.

Still worried and lonely and filled with care,
Oppressed by the same old stain,
And feel I can visit that hall no more,
Or site on that bench again.

Oh! Lassie press on in your noble cause,
With you I will ever agree,
No more to expect you to waste your smiles,
On a poor old sinner like me.

Where Old Doc
with apologies to Old Black Joe

Haddam, Conn.
Oct. 1961

Gone are the roses that beside the window blowed
Gone are the beauties from the house across the road
Call either back, no I would not if I could
For California's calling old Doc. Wood
I'm going, I'm going, back to treat that ailing stock
For I hear those Travers horses asking where old Doc.

Gone are the robins from those dear old maple trees
Flown far away to escape the coming freeze
And for the same will I leave this neighborhood
For California's calling old Doc. Wood

Chorus

Gone are those pippins from those trees beside the brook
Fell over the bough that the autumn breezes shook
Taste such in Cal. no there's none one half so good
Yet California's calling old Doc. Wood

Chorus

Gone is the schoolhouse where I learned my C.Q A's
Also the master with the good old fashion ways
Part with a sigh 'tis befitting that I should
When California's calling old Doc. Wood

Chorus

Gone are the days of my single blessedness
Found I at last one who faintly mumbled yes
Or if not that it was clearly understood
She'd go to California with old Doc. Wood
I'm going, I'm going, back to treat that ailing stock
For I hear those Travers horses asking, where old Doc.

Haddam, Conn.
Oct 1941

Where's Old Doc
with apologies to Old Black Joe

Gone are the roses that beside the window blowed
Gone are the beauties from the house across the road
Call either back, no I would not if I could
For California's calling old Doc. Wood
I'm going, I'm going, back to treat that ailing stock
for I hear those Traver horses asking where's old Doc.

Gone are the robins from those dear old maple trees
Flown far away to escape the coming freeze
And for the same will I leave this neighborhood
For California's calling old Doc. Wood

    Chorus

Gone are the pippins from those trees beside the brook
Fell from the boughs that the Autumn breezes shook
Taste such in Fall, no there's none one half so good
Yet California's calling old Doc. Wood

    Chorus

Gone is the schoolhouse where I learned my C, B, A's
Also the master with the good old fashion ways
Pass with a sigh tis befitting that I should
When California's calling old Doc. Wood

    Chorus

I'm going, I'm going
Back to treat that ailing stock.
For I hear those Travis horses asking,
Where's old Doc.

Gone are the days of my single blessedness
Found I at last one who faintly mumbled yes
Or if not that it was clearly understood
She'd go to California with old Doc. Wood
I'm going, I'm going, back to treat that ailing stock
For I hear those Traver horses asking, where's old Doc.

I'm going, I'm going
Back to treat that ailing stock.
For I hear those Traver horses asking,
Where's old Doc.

Christmas 1941

Again as in the years gone by,
To friends and loved ones dear,
I send the merry Christmas wish,
With greetings most sincere.

We try each year by different tones,
Our greetings to convey,
And bring the good old fashion news,
In some new fashion way.

The cards may be of humble type,
And simple in design,
Or be embossed with legend rare,
In tinseled beauty shine.

The purpose though, and that alone,
For which the Savior came,
Was, is, and will forever be,
Eternally the same.

Christmas 1941

Again as in the years gone by,
To friends and loved ones dear,
I send the merry Christmas wish,
With greetings most sincere.

We try each year by different tones,
Our greetings to convey,
And bring the good old fashion news,
In some new fashion way.

The cards may be of humble type,
And simple in design,
Or be embossed with legend rare,
In tinseled beauty shine.

The purpose though, and that alone,
For which the Savior came,
Was, is, and will forever be,
Eternally the same.

In the spring.   April 1942

In the spring the old man's memory,
Courses back thru lovers lane,
Plucking at the blooming roses,
Torn once more with grief and pain.

Fragrant blooms with dew bathed petals,
Deck that charming way adown,
But within the verdant foliage,
Lurks the treacherous, piercing thorn.

As I journey down this vista,
In the dreams of long ago,
Shadows hover o're my pathway,
Where the sunlight used to glow.

Shadows of those hopes departed
Shades of joys I had not known.
Tempting now in memories vision,
As I journey on alone.

Just the same, when age creeps o're me,
As it was in by gone years,
Fresh and fair from out the shadows,
Seems another rose appears.

Once again I strive to pluck it
Strain to clasp the fragrant bloom,
Then the thorns tear wicked gashes,
Sadly in the deepening gloom.

In the Spring

April 1942

In the spring the old mare's memory,
Courses back thru lovers lane,
Plucking at the blooming roses,
Torn once more with grief and pain.

Fragrant blooms with dew bathed petals,
Doth this charming way adorn,
But within the verdant foliage,
Lurks the treacherous, piercing thorn.

As I journey down this vista,
In the dreams of long ago,
Shadows hover o're my pathway,
Where the sunlight used to glow.

Shadows of those hopes departed,
Shades of joys I had not known,
Tempting now in memories vision,
As I journey on alone.

Just the same, when age creeps o're me,
As it was in by gone years,
Fresh and fair from out the shadows,
Seems another rose appears.

Once again I strive to pluck it,
Strain to clasp the fragrant bloom,
Then the thorns tear wicked gashes,
Sadly in the deepening gloom.

Thrusting in the wounds once open,
If no other portion mars,
But forever true to nature,
Tearing in the same old heart.
This is not a call for sympathy,
For someone my grief to share,
My own fault and thus deserving,
For I knew those thorns were there.

Why again must this befall me,
Why once more in this immesh,
For the thorn that wounds the spirit,
Pierces deeper than the flesh.

'Tis the breathing of the fragrance,
When the spring comes around again,
Wafted from those scented gardens,
That abound on lovers lane.

When once more, enchanted springtime,
You arrive with fragrance rare,
May it only prove a blessing,
If by chance I am not there.
Pluck me then, a bunch of roses,
Fragrant blooms of many hue,
Place them where my heart reposes,
With their petals bathed in dew.

Treacherous Piercing Thorn

Thrusting in the wounds once open,
It no other portion mars,
But forever true to nature,
Tearing in the same old scars.

This is not a call for sympathy,
For someone my grief to share,
My own fault and this deserving,
For I knew those thorns were there.

Why again must this befall me,
Why once more in this immesh,
For the thorn that wounds the spirit,
Pierces deeper than the flesh.

Tis the breathing of the fragrance,
When the spring comes around again,
Wafted from those scented gardens,
That abound on lovers lane.

When once more, enchanted springtime,
You arrive with fragrance rare,
May it only prove a blessing,
If by chance I am not there.

Pluck me then, a bunch of roses,
Fragrant blooms of marry hue,
Place them where my heart reposes,
With their petals bathed in dew.

The Cedar Chest   June 13, 1942

I now present this little chest,
To Rose, my dear loved friend,
And may the fragrance of the Rose,
With cedar fragrance blend.

And may this lovely maidens pluck,
These lines within the chest,
Remembering that to you alone,
This message is addressed.

For did you not with kindly grace,
In times of earthly strife,
Write sweetly on a fading page,
A chapter in my life.

Our lives are but an open book,
Where day by day are traced,
Some legend, chapter, verse or line,
That can not be erased.

The pleasant chapters you have wrote,
On pages near the end,
Will allways be remembered clear,
By one old faithfull friend.

June 18, 1942

The Cedar Chest

I now present this little chest,
To Rose, my dear loved friend,
And may the fragrance of the Rose,
With cedar fragrance blend.

And may this lovely maiden please,
These lines within the chest,
Remembering that to you alone,
This message is addressed,

for did you not with kindly grace,
In times of earthly strife,
Write sweetly on a fading page,
A chapter in my life.

Our lives are but an open book,
Where day by day are traced,
Some legend, chapter, verse or line,
That can not be erased.

The pleasant chapter you have wrote,
On pages near the end,
Will always be remembered dear,
By one old faithful friend.

To Rose, on her fourteenth birthday
July 28, 1942.

A happy birthday to you Rose,
I say with fond concern,
And may the same as years rollon,
Oh! many times return.

And may each happy, glad return,
Of this, your natal day,
Show one more year of worthy life,
Along the pilgrims way.

It is not fame or fortunes hight,
To which you may attain,
But in the end through worthiness,
To reach a higher plain.

The highest plain that you can reach,
Is one concidered low,
Along the path of righteousness,
"Where living waters flow."

These verses with old fashion thoughts
May seem of little worth,
So lay them down with due respect,
And join the youthfull mirth.

July 28, 1942

To Rose on her Fourteenth Birthday

A happy birthday to you Rose,
I say with fond concern,
And may the same as years roll on,
Oh! many times return.

And may each happy, glad return,
Of this, your natal day,
Show one more year of worthy life,
Along the pilgrim's way.

It is not fame or fortune's height,
To which you may attain,
But in the end through worthiness,
To reach a higher plain.

The highest plain that you can reach,
Is one considered law,
Along the path of righteousness,
"Where living waters flow."

These verses with old fashion thoughts
May seem of little worth,
so lay them down with due respect,
and join the youthful mirth.

Yet take no farther thoughts of these,
But place them safe away,
To read again in after years,
When you are old and gray.
And then this question I will ask,
What would you rather do,
Than be the fragrant bloom again,
Of nineteen forty two.

Yes take no farther thoughts of these,
But place them safe away,
To read again in after years,
When you are old and grey.

And then this question I will ask,
What would you rather do,
Than be the fragrant bloom again,
Of nineteen forty-two.

To Jensie Rusco, on her ninth birthday, Aug. 9, 1942

They tell me that on August ninth,
Of nineteen thirty three,
Our little Jensie Rusco did,
The light of day first see.

We thank the Oklahoma storks,
Who on its busy way,
Found time, this lovely little girl,
To down among us lay.

Yes Jensie was most welcome then,
And will be year by year,
So now on this, her ninth birthday,
Finds her name times more dear.

Now what can I, a gray old man,
Say to this winsome lass
What words that would be valued most
By her, as time doth pass
The Savior said long, long ago
"A little child shall lead"
So why should I, tho seeming wise,
Teach any other creed.

Now lead us, Jensie, gently on,
Until the setting sun,
Then may we hear Him fondly speak,
Those welcome words, "well done".

Aug. 9, 1942

To Jencie Rusco, on her Ninth Birthday

They tell me that on August ninth,
Of nineteen-thirty three,
Our little Jencie Rusco did,
The light of day first see.

We thank the Oklahoma stork,
Who in its busy way,
Found time, this lovely little girl,
To down among us lay.

Yes Jencie was most welcome then,
And will be year by year,
So now on this, her ninth birthday,
Finds her nine times more dear.

Now what can I, a gray old man,
Say to this winsome lass,
What words that would be valued most,
By her as time doth pass.

The Savior said long, long ago
"A little child shall lead,"
So why should I, tho seeming wise,
Teach any other creed.

Now lead us, Jencie gently on,
Until the setting sun,
Then may we hear him fondly speak,
Those welcome words, "well done."

To Jackie Russo, on her Twelfth Birthday
Oct. 11, 1942

Happy birthday dearest Jackie,
In the note I fondly send,
Hoping that throughout the future,
You will always be my friend.

On the eleventh of October,
You had chosen to appear,
Making that a happy birthday,
Nineteen thirty was the year.

Now I send my choicest greetings
To this charming little maid.
Praying that God's richest blessings
Year by year on her are laid.

This is but a simple missive,
That in simple words conveys,
Wishing many times returning,
Of your happy, glad birthday.

In the dark uncertain future,
Then wherever you may be,
While receiving birthday greetings,
Have a kindly thought of me.

Oct. 11, 1942
To Jackie Rusco, on her Twelfth Birthday

Happy birthday dearest Jackie,
Is the wish I fondly send,
Hoping that throughout the future,
You will always be my friend.

On the eleventh of October,
You had chosen to appear,
Making that a happy birthday,
Nineteen-thirty was the year.

Now I send my choicest greetings
To this charming little maid.
Praying that God's richest blessings
Year by year on her are laid.

This is but a simple missive,
That in simple words convey,
Wishing many times returning,
Of your happy, glad birthday.

In the dark uncertain future,
Then wherever you may be,
While receiving birthday greetings,
Have a kindly thought of me.

Christmas 1942

To Nellie Wilcox this is sent,
By little Loyd Wood,
Who were close neighbors long ago,
In Ponsett neighborhood.

Now we have drifted down life's stream,
Three thousand miles apart,
And time has many changes made,
Affecting head and heart.

Our thoughts turn back on Christmas day,
To Ponsett's snow clad hills,
Where coasting down those icey tracks,
We raced with childish thrills.

So now I make a Christmas wish,
That you and I could know,
One day of second childhood's joys,
As we did long ago.

Written to Mrs. Richard Warner, who was
Miss. Nellie Wilcox of Ponsett

Christmas 1942

To Nellie Wilcox this is sent,
By little Lloyd Wood,
Who were close neighbors long ago,
In Ponsett's neighborhood,

Now we have drifted down life's stream,
Three thousand miles apart,
And time has many changes made,
Affecting head and heart.

Our thoughts turn back on Christmas day,
To Ponsett's snow clad hills,
Where coasting down those icy tracks
We raced with childish thrills.

So now I make a Christmas wish,
That you and I could know,
One day of second childhood's joys,
As we did long ago.

Written to Mrs. Richard Warren, who was Miss. Nellie Wilcox of Ponsett

Feb. 14, 1943

To Dorothy, my dear beloved,
This valentine I send,
And you may claim all attributes,
Of cousin, poet, friend.
I hope that you can read these lines,
And understand it all,
For I have tried to place myself,
Behind this homely scrawl.

I am a cousin, second class,
That much is plain to see,
But as for poet, no one has,
Laid any claims on me.

Call me your poet dear beloved,
And kindly greetings send,
To cheer a poor old lonely man,
Your cousin, poet, friend.

Your valentine might be first class
Or but a penny worth,
Just any one from you would be,
The dearest one on earth.

Feb. 14, 1943

To Dorothy, my dear beloved,
This valentine I send,
And you may claim all attributes,
Of cousin, poet, friend.

I hope that you can read these lines,
And understand it all,
For I have tried to place myself,
Behind this homely scrawl.

I am a cousin, second class,
That much is plain to see,
But as for fact, no one has,
Laid any claim on me.

Call me your poet dear beloved,
And kindly greetings send,
To cheer a pour old lonely man,
Your cousin, poet, friend.

Your valentine might be first class
Or but a penny worth,
Just any one from you would be,
The dearest one on earth.

To Walk With Me   May, 27 1943

Gently blew the sweet May breezes,
And the sun had just gone down,
Basking in the early twilight,
Lay the streets of Traver Town.

Moving now from all directions,
In the evening shadows cool,
Came the people of the village,
Heading towards the Traver School.

T'was the closing of the school year,
And the happy girls and boys,
Each and all were looking forward,
To the long vacation fyst.

Now they passed with jokes and laughter,
Thru the Traver School Yard gate,
Arrayed in gay commensment costums,
Eighteen were to graduate.

With her usual friendly greetings,
Up the street came Rose Cohea
The graduates presiding student,
Of the class of forty three.

Watching her with admiration,
For in answer to my plea,
She had left her gay companions,
To come by and walk with me.

To Walk with Me

May 27, 1943

Gently blew the sweet May breezes,
And the sun had just gone down,
Basking in the early twilight,
Lay the streets of Traver Town.

Moving now from all directions,
In the evening shadows cool,
Came the people of the village,
Heading towards the Traver school.

T'was the closing of the school year,
And the happy girls and boys,
Each and all were looking forward,
To the long vacation joys.

Now they passed with jokes and laughter,
Thru the Traver Schoolyard gate,
Arrayed in gay commencement costumes,
Eighteen were to graduate.

With her usual friendly greetings,
Up the street came Rose Cohea,
The graduates presiding student,
Of the class of forty-three.

Watching her with admiration,
For in answer to my plea,
She had left her gay companions,
To come by and walk with me.

Walk with me, tonight I would not,
Need behind them all to lag,
She would time her youthfull footsteps,
To the pase my own did drag.

Youth could pause for a few moments,
With respect and due regard,
For the movements now more slowly,
Age and sickness does retard.

Youth looks forward to the future,
Age looks backward to the past,
Youth dreams on of what they will be,
Age, how much longer life will last.

Now dear Rose is starting forward,
On lifes course whate'er it be,
Could she count these moments wasted
When she paused to walk with me.

How can he the valedictorian,
Of this class to graduate,
Know if all he says farewell to,
What may happen soon or late.

But we hope these faithfull teachers,
In their pupils have instilled,
Higher aims and noble purpose,
That their dreams may be fulfilled.

Walk with me, tonight I would not,
Need behind them all to lag,
She would time her youthful footsteps,
To the pace my own did drag.

Youth could pause for a few moments,
With respect and due regard,
For the movements now more slowly,
Age and sickness does retard.

Youth looks forward to the future,
Age looks backward to the past,
Youth dreams on of what they will be,
Age, how much longer life will last.

Now dear Rose is starting forward,
On life's course what e'er it be,
Could she count these moments wasted
When she paused to walk with me.

How can he the valedictorian,
Of this class to graduate,
Know of all he says farewell to,
What may happen soon or late.

But we hope these faithful teachers,
In their pupils have instilled,
Higher aims and noble purpose,
That their dreams may be fulfilled.

School is closed, the programs ended,
Flower bedecked the students sit,
Each one holds their first diploma,
Justly they are proud of it.

Forward come their friends and parents,
To the platform where they wait,
Each in turn for farewell greetings,
And this class congratulate.

Waiting now in line to handshake,
In this crowded platform room,
One who in poetic fancy,
I had called a fragrant bloom,

All receive the same old greetings,
Eighteen in the line we see,
To the one I seem most partial,
Is the last who walked with me.

School is closed, the program ended,
Flower bedecked the students sit,
Each one holds their first diploma,
Justly they are proud of it.

Forward come their friends and parents,
To the platform where they wait,
Each in turn for farewell greetings,
And this class congratulate.

Waiting now in line to handshake,
In this crowded platform room,
One who in poetic fancy,
I had called a fragrant bloom.

All receive the same old greetings,
Eighteen in the line we see,
To the one I seem most partial,
Is the lass who walked with me.

Jackie Loves poor old Me,   Sept. 1943

Doubtings are ones for that she not traced,
Over the pages unevenly spaced,
Words so endearing as ever could be
Making it certain that Jackie loves me.
         Jackie loves poor old me.
If Jackie loves me what more could I crave,
Only the pleasure of being her slave,
For if she loves me I'll always be free,
Singing this chorus that Jackie loves me.
         Jackie loves poor old me.
Love is a treasure more precious than gold,
Come to me now when I'm feeble and old,
Late better than never, we all must agree,
When it is Jackie who says she loves me.
         Jackie loves poor old me.
What of this maiden who love has avowed,
Of her ancestors she truly is proud,
Proud of the blood of the dark Cherokee
What could that matter when Jackie loves me,
         Jackie loves poor old me.

Sept. 1943

Jackie Loves poor old Me

Doubtings are over for has she not traced,
Over the pages unevenly spaced,
Words so endearing as ever could be,
Making it certain that Jackie loves me.
    Jackie loves poor old me.

If Jackie loves me what more could I crave,
Only the pleasure of being her slave,
For if she loves me I'll always be free,
Singing this chorus that Jackie loves me.
    Jackie loves poor old me.

Love is a treasure more precious than gold,
Come to me now when I'm feeble and old,
Late better than never, we all must agree,
When it is Jackie who says she loves me.
    Jackie loves poor old me.

What of this maiden who love has avowed,
Of her ancestors she truly is proud,
Proud of the blood of the dark Cherokee
What could that matter when Jackie loves me,
    Jackie loves poor old me

Jackie loves me and I truely loves her,
How in the world could it ever occur,
Aged and youthfull, romantic to see,
I loving Jackie and Jackie loves me.
   Jackie loves poor old me.

When at last resting this weary old head,
Bathed in the tears that the willows had shed,
Close to the roots of the evergreen tree,
Dreaming forever that Jackie loves me.
   Jackie loves poor old me.

Jackie loves me and I truly love her,
How in the world could it ever occur,
Aged and youthful, romantic to see,
I loving Jackie and Jackie loves me,
     Jackie loves poor old me.

When at last resting this weary old head,
Bathed in the tears that the willows had shed,
Close to the roots of the evergreen tree,
Dreaming forever that Jackie loves me,
     Jackie loves poor old me.

To Eva on her birthday, Oct. 31, 1995

This is for my only daughter,
Dearest that could ever be,
In the future many grand ones,
May adorn my family tree.

On this last day of October,
Twenty seven years ago,
She arrived, a mite so precious,
Fondest love to her I owe.

All these years my life was brightened,
With her tender loving care,
What'ere came of joys or sorrows,
She was all ways with me there.

As the end of life grows nearer,
When and where, the time may be,
When my star of life will vanish,
I want Eva close to me.

Oct. 31, 1945

To Eva on her Birthday

This is for my only daughter,
Dearest that could ever be,
In the future many grandones,
May adorn my family tree.

On this last day of October,
Twenty seven years ago,
She arrived, a mite so precious,
Fondest love to her I owe.

All these years my life was brightened,
With her tender loving care,
What'er came of joys or sorrows,
She was all ways with me there.

As the end of life grows nearer,
When and where, the time may be,
When my star of life will vanish,
I want Eva close to me.

Walking with Joyce   Nov. 7, 1945
Tune, "Flow Gently Sweet Afton."

These lines on her birthday to Joycie I write,
This dear little Miss. had been sweet and polite,
So kind and respectfull as any could be,
Had oft in the moonlight, gone walking with me.

We walked over roads, where in days long gone by,
There, with horse and buggy, some lassie and I,
Would jog along slowly so carefree and gay,
With neither one driving, the horse knew the way.
These walks in the moonlight bring memories dear
It seems once again those old sounds I can hear,
The creak of the buggy the horses plodding feet,
Come rattling along on this old Traver street.

The old horse and buggy have been gone for years,
The hum of a motor the shifting of gears,
Are sounds so familiar now heard night and day
I choose when with Joycie, the least traveled way.

The joys of those strolls thru some forsaken trail,
With moonlight and Joycie they never can fail,
To bring back those dreams of a long, long ago,
The dreams whose fulfillment I never can know

This birthday reminder to Joycie I write,
These old fashion notions may not now delight,
But if she should keep them for fifty more years,
Then take them and read them, their meaning appears

Nov. 7, 1945

Walking with Joycie
Tune, "Flow Gently Sweet Afton"

These lines on her birthday to Joycie I write,
This clear little Miss, has been sweet and polite,
So kind and respectful as any could be,
Had oft in the moonlight, gone walking with me.

We walked over roads where in days long gone by,
There, with horse and buggy, some Lassie and I,
Would jog along slowly so carefree and gay,
With neither one driving, the horse knew the way.

These walks in the moonlight bring memories dear,
It seems once again those old sounds I can hear,
The creak of the buggy the horses plodding feet,
Come rattling along on this old Traver street.

The old horse and buggy have been gone for years,
The hum of a motor the shifting of gears,
Are sounds so familiar now heard might and day
I choose when with Joycie, the least traveled way.

The joys of those strolls thru some forsaken trail,
With moonlight and Joycie they never can fail,
To bring back those dreams of a long, long ago,
The dreams whose fulfillment I never can know.

This birthday reminder to Joycie I write,
These old fashion notions may not now delight,
But if she should keep them for fifty more years,
Then take them and read them, their meaning appears.

Now and Forever.   Nov. 14, 1945
Tune, "Annie Laurie."

This fourteenth of November, I write to L. Earl Hays,
And wish that this one may be the happiest of birthdays.
And that there may be more, beyond ten and three score,
Also with each returning, more joyfull than before.

From Arkansas she wrote me and signed it from a friend
Which was as cheering missive as any one could send.
But added to the line, was something very fine,
That it would be forever, she'd be a friend of mine.

She'd be my friend forever, the dear girl did avow,
By what I took for granted, she is my friend right now.
And that made me wonder, how could such luck accur,
That I, now and forever, have such a friend as her.

For I was old and feeble and she was young and strong,
The ending of lifes journey for me would not be long.
True friendship has no age, those who in it engage,
Write sweetly in the spirit an everlasting page.

This simple card I offer a maid of twelve years old,
The verses I have written not very much have told.
If only they express, a wish for happiness,
And that, now and forever, there will be nothing less.

Nov. 14, 1945

Now and Forever
Tune, "Annie Laurie"

This fourteenth of November, I write to L Earl Hays,
And wish that this one may be the happiest of birthdays,
And that there may be more, beyond ten and thrice score,
Also with each returning, more joyful than before.

From Arkansas she wrote me and signed it from a friend,
Which was as cheering missive as any one could find,
But added to the line, was something very fine,
That it would be forever, she'd be a friend of mine.

She'd be my friend forever, the dear girl did avow,
By that I took for granted, she is my friend right now,
And that made me wonder, how could such luck occur,
That I, now and forever, have such a friend as her.

For I was old and feeble and she was young and strong,
The ending of life's journey for me would not be long.
True friendship has no age, those who in it engage,
Write sweetly in the spirit an everlasting prize.

This simple card I offer a maid of twelve years old,
The verses I have written not very much have told.
If only they express, a wish for happiness,
And that, now and forever, there will be nothing less.

Christmas 1945

They tell me now when I am old,
There is no Santa Claus,
I argue with them one and all,
That long ago there was.

The legend of good old St. Nick
With reindeers and his sleighs,
The children with steadfast belief,
In those old fashion days,

Took stockings every Christmas eve,
Tip toeing in so still,
And hung them by the chimney place,
For Santa Claus to fill.

No longer can that friend of old,
Dear to each childish heart,
Perform the wonders that he did,
The people are to smart.

With every form of coal oil stove,
Electric, and butane,
With chimnies all gone out of date,
What entry could he gain.

The world now in these modern times
By moving on so fast,
Has made of poor old Santa Claus,
A spirit of the past.

Christmas 1945

They tell me now when I am old,
There is no Santa Claus,
I argue with them one and all,
That long there was.

The legend of good old St. Nick,
With reindeers and his sleighs,
The children with steadfast belief,
In those old fashion days,

Took stockings every Christmas eve,
Tiptoeing in so still,
And hung them by the chimney place,
For Santa Claus to fill.

No longer can that friend of old,
Dear to each childish heart,
Perform the wonders that he did,
The people are too smart.

With every form of coal oil stove,
Electric, and butane,
With chimnies all gone out of date,
What entry could he gain.

The world now in these modern times
By moving on so fast,
Has made of poor old Santa Claus,
A spirit of the past.

To Jencie Rusco   Feb. 23, 1946

The day of valentines has passed,
And I sent none to you,
What reason was there to neglect,
A friend so kind and true.

It seemed to be but carelessness,
So now I make amend,
And send this friendly little card,
To Jencie dear, my friend.

I ask forgivness now of you,
For sending this so late,
And next year I will shurely try,
To be more up to date.

Now this is not a valentine,
But just a substitute,
It is the best that I can do,
I hope you'll think it cute.

And be my valentine this year,
Thru nineteen faty six,
And next year I'll try not to be,
In such a lazy fix.

Feb. 23, 1946

To Jencie Rusco

The day of valentines has passed,
And I sent none to you.
What reason was there to neglect,
A friend so kind and true.

It seemed to be but carelessness,
So now I make amend,
And send this friendly little card,
To Jencie dear, my friend.

I ask forgiveness now of you,
For sending this so late,
And next year I will surely try,
To be more up to date.

Now this is not a valentine,
but just a substitute,
It is the best that I can do,
I hope you'll think it cute.

And be my valentine this year,
Thru nineteen forty six,
And next year I'll try not to be,
In such a lazy fix.

Hello! Jackie and thank you,
Is what I now must say.
And I do realy mean it,
In a most friendly way.

You were so kind to send me,
That lovely valentine,
And say its to my sweetheart,
I kissed on every line.

This world, the verses said dear,
Is realy very small,
The others ones around us,
Din't count for much at all.
If that were realy ~~it~~ ~~true~~ so dear,
T'would be my dreams come true,
With no one else to share dear,
The joy of loving you.

This card that I am sending,
Is from an old boy friend,
I hope this trusting friendship,
Will never see an end.

Hello! Jackie and thank you,
Is what I now must say.
And I do really mean it,
In a most friendly way.

You were so kind to send me,
That lovely valentine,
And say it's to my sweetheart,
I kissed on every line.

This world, the verses said dear,
Is really very small,
The other ones around us,
Don't count for much at all.

If this were really so dear,
T'would be my dreams come true,
With no one else to share dear,
The joy of loving you.

This card that I am sending,
Is from an old boy friend,
I hope this trusting friendship,
will never see an end.

Three little girls and I
Mar. 31, 1946

Three little girls and I, yes
Three little girls and I;
Two show in the picture,
While one snapped the picture,
With sun in the noon day sky.

Three little maids so lovely,
Close by my side appear.
My wishes fulfilling,
Stand proudly and willing,
My lonely old life to cheer.

I was four times a grandpa,
My hair was white as snow.
These dear girls befriended,
With my age they blended,
Their radiant childish glow.

One little girl, Juanita,
Beautifull dark brown hair.
At my left standing,
Attention demanding,
The photograph shows her there.

Mar. 31, 1946

Three little girls and I

Three little girls and I, yes
Three little girls and I;
Two show in the mixture,
While one snapped the picture,
With sun in the noonday sky.

Three little maids so lovely,
Close by my side appear.
My wishes fulfilling,
Stand proudly and willing,
My lonely old life to cheer.

I was four times a grandpa,
My hair was white as snow.
These dear girls befriended.
With my age they blended,
Their radiant childish glow.

One little girl, Juanita,
Beautiful dark brown hair.
At my left standing,
Attention demanding,
The photograph shows her there.

One little girl was Melba,
Stands closely at my right.
Oh! who could be sweeter,
Than she and Juanita,
T'was realy a pleasing sight.

Then Evelyn snapped the picture,
The last named of the three.
The credit deserving,
All three of us serving,
Then taking her pose with me.

Three little girls and I, yes
Three little girls so gay.
If we should discover,
That they had no lover,
I gladly would serve that way.

The three little girls
Juanita Yager
Melba Moore
Evelyn Scroggins

One little girl was Melba,
Stands closely at my right.
Oh! who could be sweeter,
Than she and Juanita,
T'was really a pleasing sight.

Then Evelyn snapped the picture,
The last named of the three.
The credit deserving,
All three of us serving,
Then taking her pose with me.

Three little girls and I, yes.
Three little girls so gay.
If we should discover,
That they had no lover,
I gladly would serve that way.

The three little girls
Juanita Yagers
Melba Moore
Evelyn Scroggins

To Dorothy, April 21, 1949

Easter greetings that you sent me,
From the one I love so dear,
Was a most uplifting missive,
One that I had longed to hear.

Tho the message was commercial,
Printed on a card for sale,
Any one could buy and send it,
To another thru the mail,
I accept it as its written,
Easter greetings of your own,
And return in equal measure,
The same wish the card has shown.

To Dorothy

April 21, 1946

Easter greetings that you sent me,
From the one I love so dear,
Was a most uplifting missive,
One that I had longed to hear.

Tho the message was commercial,
Printed on a card for sale,
Any one could buy and send it,
To another thru the mail,

I accept it as its written,
Easter greetings of your own,
And return in equal measure,
The same wish the card has shown.

To Dolores Morales   May 1946

This little book I now present,
Tells how to draw a tree.
And it is given with the hope,
You may remember me.

The picture of a locust tree,
I hope you'll learn to draw,
And hanging from a lower limb,
The girl so many saw.

"Oh! Oh Wood, come help me down,
I'll tumble and get hurt,"
I tried to help her and we both,
Went sprawling in the dirt.

Remember how the children laughed?
And jumped around with glee,
For nothing else but that, I trust,
You will remember me

May 1946

To Dorothy Morales

This little book I now present,
Tells how to draw a tree.
And it is given with the hope,
You may remember me.

The picture of a locust tree,
I hope you'll learn to draw,
And hanging from a lower limb,
The girl so many saw.

"Oh! Mr. Wood, come help me down,
I'll tumble and get hurt,"
I tried to help her and we both,
Went sprawling in the dirt.

Remember how the children laughed?
And jumped around with glee,
For nothing else but that, I trust,
You will remember me.

Tune, My old Kentucky Home   May 23, 1946

The May breeze blows on the dusty Traver streets,
'Tis nearing the last day of spring,
We graduates of the class of forty six,
In the program now our song will sing.
We welcome all of our relatives and friends,
Our school days in Traver are o'er,
We say good by to all efforts of the past,
For we study in this school no more.

To our worthy teachers we offer this refrain,
And extend our thanks for their guiding on the way,
As their debtors we must e'er remain.

As we greet our friends in closing of this school,
Sweet memories before us arise,
Our thoughts turn back to classmate fellowships,
That are bound with many tender ties.
They are not confined to members of our class,
But to classes of days gone by,
Also those who are following behind,
And our teachers we can not decry.

May 23, 1946

Tune, My Old Kentucky Home

The May breeze blows on the dusty Traver streets,
T'is nearing the last day of spring,
We graduates of the class of forty six,
In the program now our song will sing.

We welcome all of our relatives and friends,
Our school days in Traver are o'er,
We say good by to all efforts of the past,
For we study in this school no more.

To our worthy teachers we offer this refrain,
And extend our thanks for their guiding on the way,
As their debtors we must e're remain.

As we greet our friends in closing of this school,
Sweet memories before us arise.
Our thoughts turn back to classmate fellowships,
That are bound with many tender ties.
They are not confined to members of our class,
But to classes of days gone by,
Also those who are following behind,
And our teachers we can not deny.

With a backward glance we turn and face the world,
Before us our problems all lie,
We can not tell what the future has in store,
Hoping for a sweeter by and by.
We give our place to the class of forty seven,
Who answer the call of the bell,
That rings no more for the class of forty six,
So to Traver school we bid farewell.

Now our friends and neighbors, all those from far and near,
Give a strong hand clap for the class of forty six,
And its memory we will hold most dear.

Written for the graduating class of Traver School 1946, but rejected by the principal. It was said that the class wished to sing it as their closing song

Treacherous Piercing Thorn

With a backward glance we turn and face the world,
Before us our problems all lie,
We can not tell what the future has in store,
Hoping for a sweeter by and by.
We give our place to the class of forty seven,
Who answer the call of the bell,
That rings no more for the class of forty six,
So to Traver School we bid farewell.

Now our friends and neighbors, all those from far and near,
Give a strong hand clap for the classy forty six,
And its memory we will hold most dear.

Written for the graduating class of Traver School 1946, but rejected by the principal. It was said that the class wished to sing it as their closing song.

A girl less day   June 20, 1946

    Who'll be the first
      Who'll be the first
Who'll be the first to call on me
Who'll be the first to sit upon my lap
In the shade of the locust tree
    Who'll be the first
      Who'll be the first
Who'll be the first to call on me
Who'll be the first to dangle from the bar
In the shade of the locust tree

    No body came
      No body came
No body came to call on me
None in my lap or dangled from the bar
In the shade of the locust tree
    A girl less day
      A girl less day
No lassie came to call on me
Lonely I sat while ants crawled on the bar
In the shade of the locust tree

June 20, 1946

A girl less day

    Who'll be the first
    Who'll be the first
Who'll be the first to call on me
Who'll be the first to sit upon my lap
In the shade of the locust tree
    Who'll be the first
    Who'll be the first
Who'll be the first to call on me
Who'll be the first to dangle from the bar
In the shade of the locust tree
    No body came
    No body came
No body came to call on me
None in my lap or dangled from the bar
In the shade of the locust tree
    A girl less day
    A girl less day
No lassie came to call on me
Lonely I sat while ants crawled on the bar
In the shade of the locust tree

To Martha Ann, on her tenth birthday
July 17, 1941

To a lovely little maiden,
Who has reached the age of ten,
On her birthday I will offer,
As a gift this fountain pen.

With its point I trace this missive,
With an old and pattering hand,
May a friendship hold between us,
Firmer than a golden band.

We can only judge the future,
By the happenings of the past,
And by those I feel most certain,
That my hopes are bound to last.

Try this pen and if you care to,
Write to me some simple line,
That reflects on by gone pleasures,
That were yours and also mine.

July 17, 1946

To Martha Ann on her Tenth Birthday

To a lonely little maiden,
Who has reached the age of ten,
On her birthday I will offer,
As a gift this fountain pen.

With its point I trace this missive,
With an old and faltering hand,
May a friendship hold between us,
Firmer than a golden band.

We can only judge the future,
By the happenings of the past,
And by those I feel most certain,
That my hopes are bound to last.

Try this pen and if you care to,
Write to me some simple line,
That reflects on by gone pleasures,
That were yours and also mine.

References

Annie Laurie, subject of Scotland's best-known love song, was daughter of the first Baronet of Maxwelton. Annie (Anna) Laurie and William Douglas may have had a fleeting romance. We do know that Anna's family would not consent to any marriage. Whatever happened, the lovers went their separate ways. Douglas wrote his tuneless two-verse song in the first years of the 18th century, probably at his castle at Fingland. Alicia Spottiswoode write the current version, considerably altered the original and added a third verse. She set it to a tune that she had earlier composed for the old ballad Kempye Kaye.

The Balm of Gilead was a sap drawn from cuts in trees native to Gilead (in ancient Israel). It was used by Skilled physicians in the region to treat patients. In verses such as Jeremiah 46:11 it is used a metaphor for the ability of Jesus Christ to heal sin.

Dobbin's Diner -- Dobbin, originated in 1596, means farm horse and Diners were train cars made into restaurants (Charles Wood). I suspect 'Dobbins Diner' was the name of a diner in Traver.

Flow Gently Sweet Afton was written by Robert Burns in 1791. It appeared in the Scots Musical Museum in 1792. Alexander Hume composed the music. You can find the words to the poem at http://www.recmusic.org/lieder/b/burns/britten92.5.html. Robert Burns, the "National Bard of Scotland" was born in Alloway, Scotland in 1759. His first book, Poems, was an immediate success and across England and Scotland he was seen a great "peasant-poet." He later helped with anthologies that were essential in preserving key songs from Scotland's past such as "My Luve is Like a Red Red Rose" and "Auld Land Syne." His poems —most written in Scots— celebrate Scottish culture, farm life and class and religious differences. He also wrote ballads, letters and over

300 songs before passing away from a terminal case of heart disease at the age of thirty-seven.

Stephen C. Foster was born on July 4, 1826 in Pennsylvania. At seven, he came across a flute—he'd never seen one before— and mastered it before leaving the store. At sixteen he published his first composition. In spite of only one trip to the south during his life (on a riverboat), he had an instinctive feel for the pace and atmosphere of life below the Mason-Dixon Line. Many of his most loved and enduring songs concern life on the plantation, such as the ones referenced here and Camptown Races. Other classics he composed in his short but brilliant life include Jeannie With the Light Brown Hair, Beautiful Dreamer and Hard Times. Over his life he wrote over 200 songs. An accidental fall in a hotel room during a bout of fever sent proved to be fatal and he later in 1864 he died.

Haddam (Middlesex County), Connecticut is located near the coast and, uniquely, straddles the Connecticut River. The land for what would become Haddam was purchased from the Indians in May 1662 and Haddam itself was incorporated in 1668. Before the end of the year, the power of the river was tapped with the town's first grist mill. Soon, textile, tannery, and distillery businesses lined the river and four ferries serviced the area. The Connecticut River was noted for a yearly shad run so plentiful that disgruntled farmhands insisted that they be served shad no more than five times a week in their contracts. Granite valuable for paving stones was quarried in the area and shipped from Rock Landing to pave significant portions of New Orleans and Savannah. Today Haddam is a residential community of 7,800 people (2007) and site of the Connecticut Yankee Atomic Power Plant.

My Old Kentucky Home was written by Stephen C. Foster in 1853 and may have been inspired by Uncle Tom's Cabin

(Harriet Beecher Stowe, 1851). The first draft in Foster's workbook was called "Poor Uncle Tome, Good Night." It became the Kentucky State Song in 1928.

OLD BLACK JOE was a folk song written in 1860 by Stephen C. Foster and popular during the Civil War. It's been performed by a long list of artists including Van Morrison, Jerry Lee Lewis and the Glen Miller Orchestra.

PIPPINS are any of a number of different "roundish or oblate" varieties of apple (Websters).

PONSETT is the neighborhood immediately west of the center of Haddam (Middlesex County), Connecticut.

Lyric Sheets

2
Her brow is like the snaw drift
Her throat is like the swan;
Her face it is the fairest
That e'er the sun shone on.
That e'er the sun shone on,
And dark blue is her e'e:
And for bonnie Annie Laurie
I'd lay me doune and dee.

3
Like dew on the gowan lying
Is the fa' o' her fairy feet;
And like winds in summer sighing,
Her voice is low and sweet.
Her voice is low and sweet
And she is a' the world to me;
And for bonnie Annie Laurie
I'd lay me doune and dee

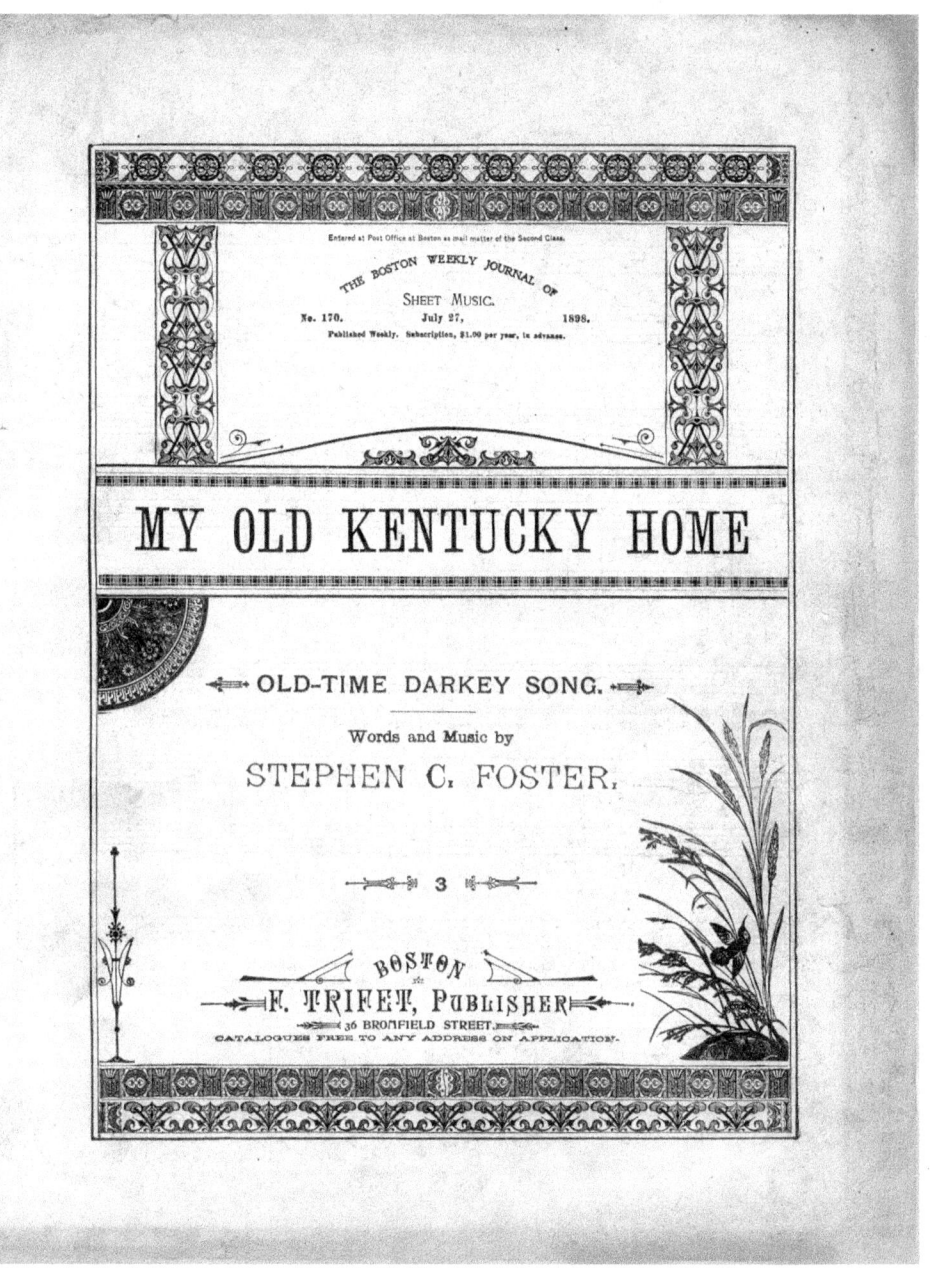

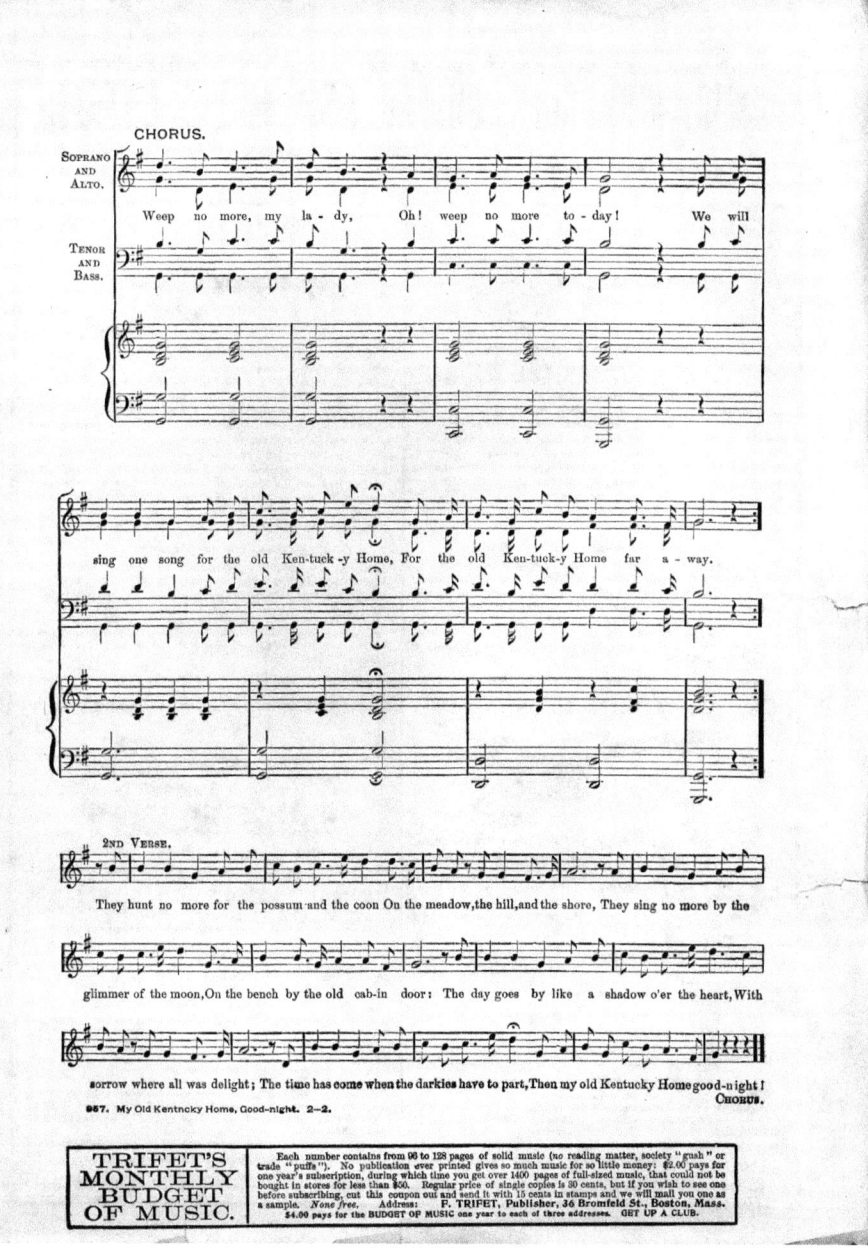

BANJO, MANDOLIN, GUITAR AND VIOLIN OUTFITS.

THE MOST VALUE, FOR THE LEAST MONEY, EVER OFFERED TO PURCHASERS OF MUSICAL INSTRUMENTS.
Each and Every Outfit Guaranteed to be as Represented and if not Perfectly Satisfactory can be Returned after One Weeks Trial and Money will be Refunded.

ACADEMY BANJO OUTFIT.

This is an up-to-date Standard BANJO,

Producing a tone that is rich, brilliant and strong. The scale is absolutely perfect. Rim and top hoop made of German silver, fitted with 16 heavily nickel-plated brackets nicely made, a fine even white calf head, thoroughly stretched. A *cherry* stained arm, dowel and inside rim beautifully shaped and polished; studs and braces made of the best steel. Fancy carved veneered scroll and ebonized fingerboard, fretted with 18 German silver frets, five real ebony pegs dotted with pearl, and the latest style ebony tailpiece finely carved and engraved and fastened on to the banjo with a neat, nickel-plated adjustable rod and end bracket. A full set of the finest quality German strings, a finely cut, latest pattern maple bridge, and a strong laquered brass wrench for tightening brackets.

A case-shaped green baize Banjo BAG,

Flannel lined, fitted with three heavy brass snap fasteners, a well made and strong handle, a pocket on inside to hold extra strings, &c., together with the latest Banjo BOOK, containing complete instructions with a great many exercises and collection of popular music.

The Academy BANJO OUTFIT, complete, by express, for $5.00, or will be given FREE for a club of NINE yearly subscribers, at $1.00 each, to the WEEKLY JOURNAL OF SHEET MUSIC.

ACADEMY GUITAR OUTFIT.

The ACADEMY GUITAR,

Has that wonderfully deep, round and strong tone, so much desired in instruments of this kind, full standard size, the back and sides are built of rosewood stained birch, splendidly finished, neck of the same wood and finish, top or sound board has a white holly edge inlaid with colored woods, with many colored strips of inlaying around the sound hole, the head is nicely cut and fitted, solid rosewood fingerboard inlaid with pearl positions, 18 German silver frets and perfect scale, fancy figured rosewood bridge with ivory saddle and six nicely adjusted pins, an even and brilliant set of strings and an ebony string nut. Either steel, compound, gut or silk strings can be used on the Academy Guitar.
This instrument is recommended as being first-class in every particular.

A green felt box-shaped BAG,

Fitted with pocket for strings, &c., and having the brass snap fasteners, is furnished with this outfit, and a very good instruction book, containing rudiments, exercises, and a number of very good guitar solos and songs.

The Academy GUITAR OUTFIT, complete, by express, for $5.00, or will be given FREE for a club of NINE yearly subscribers, at $1.00 each, to the WEEKLY JOURNAL OF SHEET MUSIC.

UNIVERSITY MANDOLIN OUTFIT.

The Above is a True Picture of the Justly Celebrated UNIVERSITY MANDOLIN,

One of the finest of club and solo instruments, It is much easier to hold than the other styles of mandolins, especially so for Ladies and Children, and the easiest to learn how to play. Built to stand in any climate. The old fashioned bowl shaped mandolin does not compare with it either in quality of tone, beauty of outline, workmanship or finish.
The tone is sweet, clear and powerful, both on the wound, as well as on the treble strings; the back, sides and neck is made of the best quality genuine San Domingo mahogany, beautifully polished; the top is made of straight grain, clear Swiss deal, oval sound-hole, with a border of seven layers of various colored woods, the scroll is neatly shaped and tapered, highly finished ebony fingerboard, inlaid with pearl positions and fretted with 17 German silver frets. Scale is accurately drawn, beautifully inlaid tortoise shell design guard plate, handsomely shaped lyre design tailpiece and sleeve protector nickel plated. The finest quality laquered brass machine head, with tempered steel screws and rods, ivory pattern buttons, ebony bridge, saddle and heel; this mandolin is strung with eight of the highest grade nickel steel strings.

Real Tortoise Shell Plectrum.

The University Mandolin will compare favorably with a $25.00 mandolin of any other make.
A felt bag, green in color and box-shaped, made to fit mandolin perfectly, having a pocket to contain strings, picks, &c., and fastening with laquered brass snap catches.
Also, a Book, containing complete instructions and a fine collection of studies and melodies.

This OUTFIT complete, by express, on receipt of $5.00, or will be given FREE for a club of NINE yearly subscribers, at $1.00 each, to WEEKLY JOURNAL OF SHEET MUSIC.

CREMONA VIOLIN OUTFIT.

A Beautiful Stradivarius Model Cremonese VIOLIN,

With a sweet and most powerful tone, the color is a rich golden amber brown varnish, handsomely shaded on finely marked old wood, the outline is graceful and the workmanship excellent; the pegs, tailpiece and pin, and fingerboard are made of the best ebony, finished in first class style; the E, A, D and G strings, are the finest quality Russian gut, gauged in proportion one with the other; the bridge is nicely figured maple properly cut and fitted.
This artist violin is sent you in perfect condition for immediate use.

A Handsome Brazilwood, Full Length BOW,

Nicely tapered and splendidly balanced, real ebony frog trimmed with German silver and pearl, with silvered lapping around end of bow.
This is a business bow, well haired, beautifully made and thoroughly reliable.

A Basswood Violin CASE,

Modern shape, ebonized and highly polished, inside fitted with compartments to hold strings, rosin, etc. and shaped to fit curve of the violin, bow pocket for holding bow firmly in place, the lock, catches, hinges, rosettes and handle are made of laquered brass, red felt lining for violin to rest upon, and a complete
Instruction Book containing exercises and over 550 pieces of standard music, and a box of very good Rosin is also included.

This Splendid VIOLIN OUTFIT, that any musician might be proud to own, complete in every detail, by express on receipt of $5.00, or will be given FREE for a club of NINE yearly subscribers, at $1.00 each, to WEEKLY JOURNAL OF SHEET MUSIC.

Remit by Draft, Money Order or Cash (In Registered Letter) at our risk, and Address all Orders to

 F. TRIFET, 36 Bromfield Street, BOSTON, MASS.

Maps

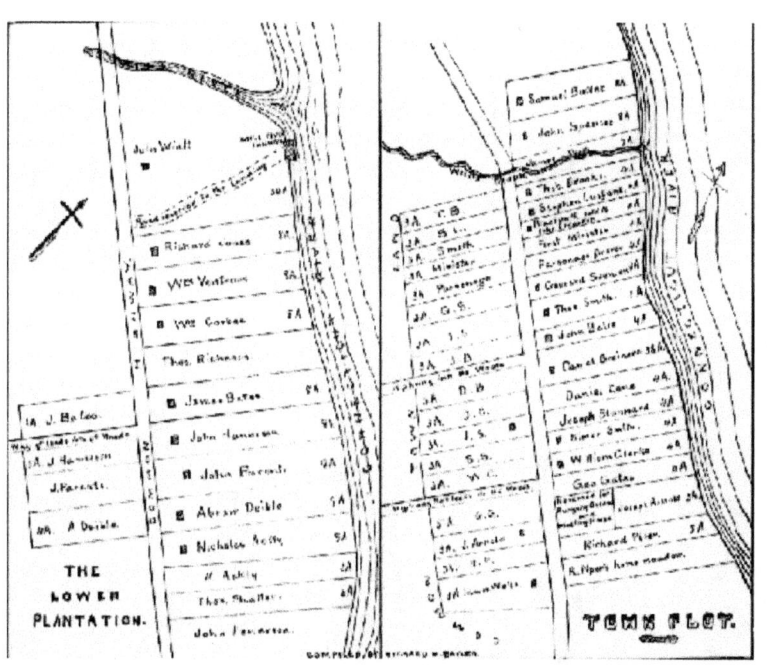

Town of Haddam Founder's Map

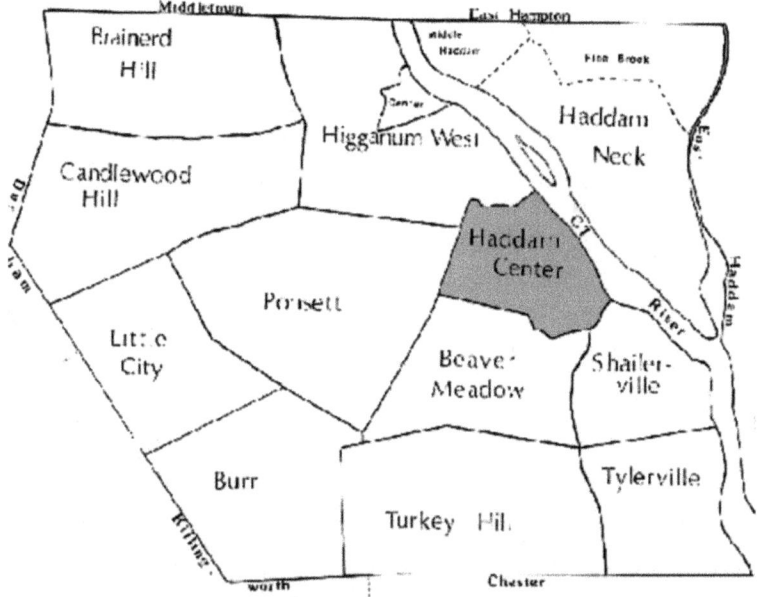

Town of Haddam Historic Districts

Lloyd Nelson Wood is one a list of poets in an extended clan with last names like Wood and Thornburg centered in Fresno, California. Lloyd Nelson Wood's surviving poetry was written during the 1940's and is contained in this collection. Lloyd Nelson Wood was born in Haddam (Middlesex County), Connecticut to Charles Anson and Mary L. Wood in 1879. He moved to California and studied at the University of California San Francisco, but managed to get out of town before it burned in 1906. He married Mary Anna Crook in 1911 and worked as a Veterinarian.

www.ingramcontent.com/pod-product-compliance
Lightning Source LLC
LaVergne TN
LVHW051501070426
835507LV00022B/2880